CELEB SOCCER STAR

GEOFF BARKER

SEA-TO-SEA
Mankato Collingwood London

This edition first published in 2012 by

Sea-to-Sea Publications
Distributed by Black Rabbit Books
P.O. Box 3263, Mankato, Minnesota 56002

Copyright © Sea-to-Sea Publications 2012

Printed in China

All rights reserved.

9 8 7 6 5 4 3 2

Published by arrangement with the
Watts Publishing Group Ltd, London.

A CIP catalog record for this book
is available from the Library of Congress.

ISBN: 978-1-59771-334-4

Planning and production by Discovery Books Limited
Managing editor: Laura Durman
Editor: Clare Hibbert
Designer: D.R. ink
Picture research: Colleen Ruck

Photo acknowledgments: Getty Images: cover (Glyn Kirk/AFP), pp 4 (Mark Thompson), 6–7 (Odd Andersen/AFP), 7 (Paul Gilham), 8–9 (Alex Livesey), 13 (Alex Livesey), 14–15 (Alex Livesey), 16 (Antonio Scorza/AFP), 20 (Ross Kinnaird), 22 (Walter Astrada/AFP), 23 (Josep Lago/AFP), 25 (Paul Gilham), 28 (Jeff J. Mitchell), 29 (David Cannon); Rex Features: pp 11 (Giuliano Bevilacqua), 12 (Simon Stacpoole), 17 (Action Press), 18, 21 (Rotello), 27 (Sipa Press); Shutterstock Images: pp 1 and 10 (Jonathan Larsen), 3 (Stawek), 5 (Sportsphotographer.eu), 19 and 31 (Alexander Gordeyev), 26 (Adam Gasson).

Every attempt has been made to clear copyright. Should there be any inadvertent omission, please apply to the Publishers for rectification.

To the best of its knowledge, the Publisher believes the facts in this book to be true at the time of going to press. However, due to the nature of celebrity, it is impossible to guarantee that all the facts will still be current at the time of reading.

February 2011
RD/6000006415/001

Note to parents and teachers: Every effort has been made by the Publishers to ensure that the web sites in this book are suitable for children, that they are of the highest educational value, and that they contain no inappropriate or offensive material. However, because of the nature of the Internet, it is impossible to guarantee that the contents of these sites will not be altered. We strongly advise that Internet access is supervised by a responsible adult.

CONTENTS

How to Be a Good Player	JOHN TERRY	4
Rising Stars	THEO WALCOTT	6
Team Captain	STEVEN GERRARD	8
Silky Skills	CRISTIANO RONALDO	10
Overseas Flair	FERNANDO TORRES	12
Playing for Your Country	WAYNE ROONEY	14
The World Cup	RONALDO	16
Big Bucks	DAVID BECKHAM	18
Showbiz Lifestyle	LANDON DONOVAN	20
Role Models	SAMUEL ETO'O	22
Women's Soccer	MARTA VIEIRA DA SILVA	24
Fans' Favorites	RYAN GIGGS	26
Life After Soccer	ALEXI LALAS	28
Glossary		30
Further Information		31
Index		32

HOW TO BE A GOOD PLAYER

fact

John Terry beat off fierce competition from Steven Gerrard and Rio Ferdinand to become England captain in 2008.

"I realize soccer's my life and I have got one chance at it."

Terry in action during a qualifying game for the 2010 FIFA World Cup.

Terry playing for Chelsea during the Champions League final in Moscow in 2008.

CELEB BIO

Date of birth **December 7, 1980**
Place of birth **Barking, Greater London, UK**
Position **Center back**
Height **6 ft. 2 in. (1.87 m)**
Biggest achievements **Chelsea captain in 2004–05 when Chelsea won Premiership; voted PFA Players' Player of the Year**
Training **Chelsea youth system beginning age 14**
Inspirational figures **Gianfranco Zola, Bobby Moore**

JOHN TERRY

Soccer players are great athletes. Soccer is a very competitive sport, and only the very best stand a chance of making it. Top players like John Terry have to be tough, as well as talented.

WILL TO WIN

The best players, like John Terry, remain focused for the whole match. They love their club and play with passion, determined to win every game. Soccer players also need to be disciplined and play by the rules. Being sent off for a foul lets down the whole team.

TEAM SPIRIT

Players have to pull together, work as a team, and try to follow the manager's game plan. Strikers focus on attack, trying to score a goal in the opponents' net. Defenders try to cancel out the threat of the opposing team's strikers.

NO NONSENSE

Chelsea center back John Terry is a no-nonsense defender. He reads the game well and makes brave challenges. He is brilliant in the air, either clearing the ball or scoring vital goals with his head from set plays.

LEADER OF MEN

John Terry is mentally very strong. Thanks to his hard work and determination, he has authority on the playing field and in the dressing room. His teammates in the Chelsea club and the national team of England respect him. As captain of both club and country, he leads by example and motivates his players.

RISING STARS

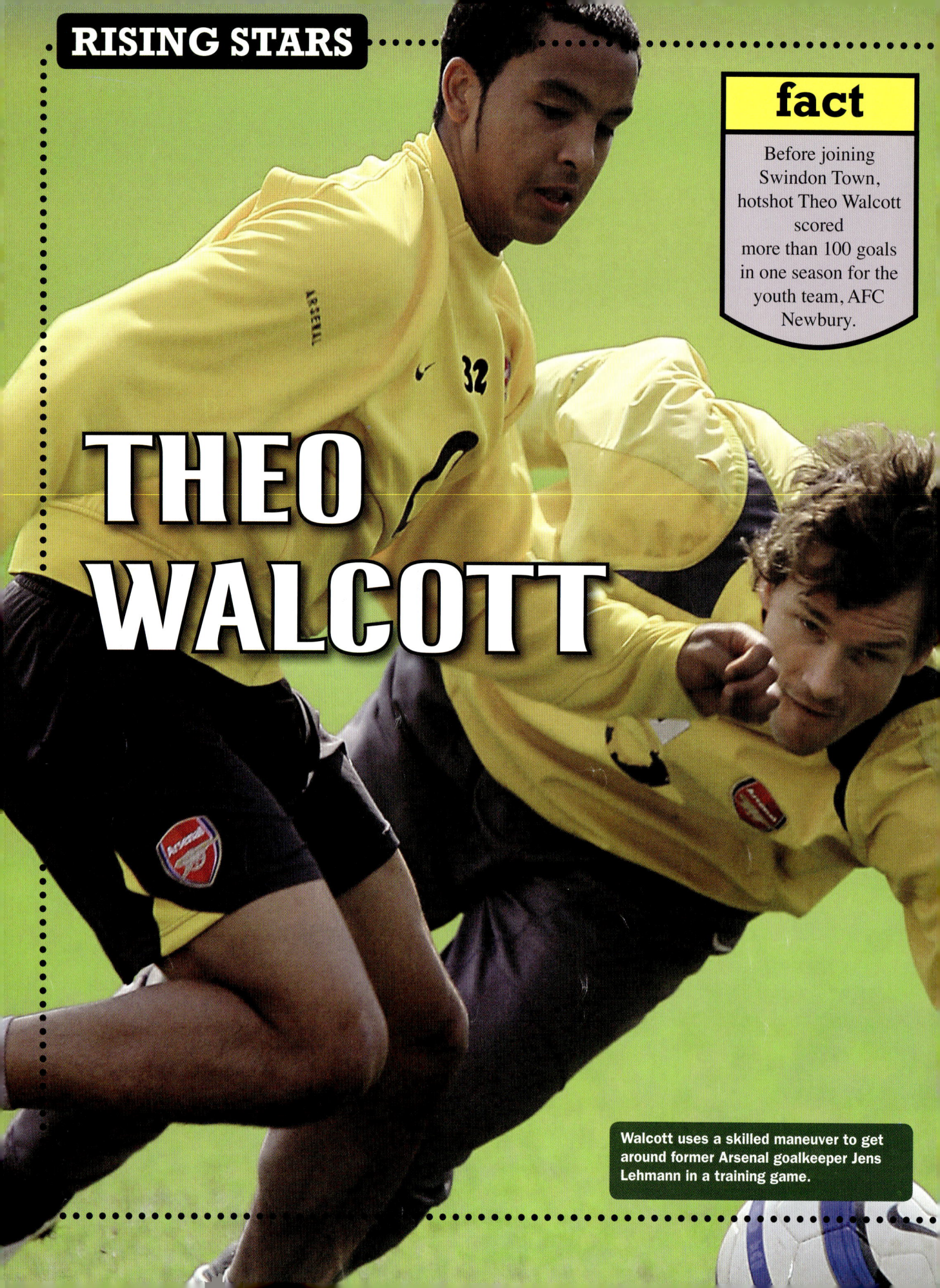

THEO WALCOTT

fact

Before joining Swindon Town, hotshot Theo Walcott scored more than 100 goals in one season for the youth team, AFC Newbury.

Walcott uses a skilled maneuver to get around former Arsenal goalkeeper Jens Lehmann in a training game.

A new generation of young players is emerging. Bright young stars like Theo Walcott develop their talents at training schemes set up by Premiership and League clubs—soccer academies and centers of excellence.

THROUGH THE RANKS

Most players join a local club's academy around the age of nine. At 16, a small handful of hopefuls are selected to carry on and join youth training schemes, which usually last three years—but most youngsters don't make it.

EARLY YEARS

Exceptional talents such as Theo Walcott shine as soccer players at an early age. Walcott played at youth level for AFC Newbury, Swindon Town, and Southampton. He broke into the Southampton first team in 2005 aged 16 and attracted the attention of the top clubs.

SIGNING FOR ARSENAL

Arsenal, which has a reputation for developing young talent, bought Walcott in 2006. Walcott has skill, trickery, and raw pace. He uses these qualities to outwit hardened professionals in a tough Premiership.

VERY BRIGHT FUTURE

Theo Walcott looks capable of becoming a great player. He is able to stay level-headed, even when he is playing a really crucial game. In only his second competitive start for England in 2008, he scored a memorable hat trick against Croatia in an important 2010 World Cup qualifying game.

Walcott observes play during a UEFA Under-21 Championship qualifying game between Portugal and England.

CELEB BIO

Date of birth March 16, 1989

Place of birth Stanmore, Greater London, UK

Position Winger

Height 5 ft. 9 in. (1.75 m)

Biggest achievement Being picked for the 2006 World Cup squad; becoming the youngest player to score a hat trick for England (in 2008)

Training Swindon Town and Southampton youth teams

Inspirational figures Robbie Fowler, Michael Owen, Thierry Henry

> "I have been around for quite a long time... but I am still learning my trade."

TEAM CAPTAIN

STEVEN GERRARD

> **fact**
> Gerrard was voted second in a poll to find the best player for Liverpool ever—only the great Kenny Dalglish was ahead of him.

The club manager picks the team and sets out a game plan. But during the game, it is the team captain who leads the players on the playing field. The captain tries to motivate his players to perform at their very best.

LEADING BY EXAMPLE

Soccer captains are leaders. They help enable 11 individuals to play together as a team. They must lead by example, showing energy and drive on the field. As club captain, Steven Gerrard is the heart and soul of Liverpool's team.

PRODUCT OF YOUTH TRAINING

Local youngster Gerrard joined Liverpool's youth academy when he was nine. He made his debut for Liverpool Football Club age 18 in 1998. Liverpool FC saw that the skinny young midfielder had leadership qualities. In 2003, he replaced Sami Hyypia as club captain.

DRIVING FORCE

Even though Gerrard felt out of his depth playing in his first season, he quickly settled in. As he grew stronger, he became a fierce tackler. Gerrard developed a dynamic playing style, dominating the midfield and driving on his team. He also contributes vital goals during a season, many of them blasted in from outside the box.

FIGHTING BACK

Liverpool have an inspirational captain in Gerrard. In the 2005 Champions League final, the team was behind 3–0 at half-time against AC Milan. Gerrard scored with a header to lead an incredible fightback. Within six minutes, the score was 3–3! Liverpool won on penalties and Gerrard, as captain, lifted the Champions League trophy. It was an unforgettable moment.

"I've got absolutely no intention of ever going to play for another club."

CELEB BIO

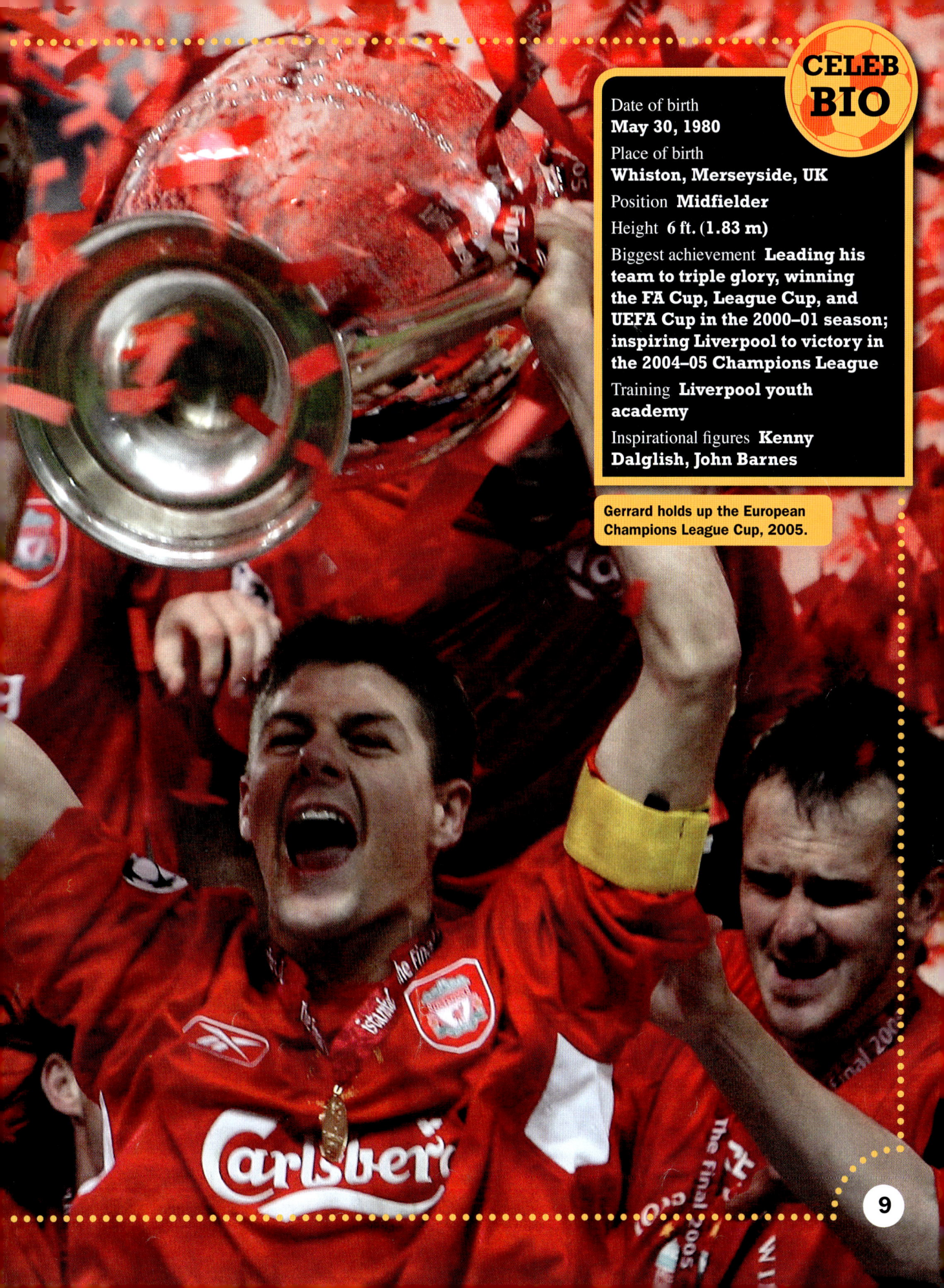

Date of birth **May 30, 1980**

Place of birth **Whiston, Merseyside, UK**

Position **Midfielder**

Height **6 ft. (1.83 m)**

Biggest achievement **Leading his team to triple glory, winning the FA Cup, League Cup, and UEFA Cup in the 2000–01 season; inspiring Liverpool to victory in the 2004–05 Champions League**

Training **Liverpool youth academy**

Inspirational figures **Kenny Dalglish, John Barnes**

Gerrard holds up the European Champions League Cup, 2005.

9

SILKY SKILLS

CRISTIANO RONALDO

Premiership soccer is all about power and pace. Fans also love to see skillful players like Cristiano Ronaldo showing their special tricks and flicks—as long as they work. One mistake and the team can fall behind.

Ronaldo in action for Portugal in a UEFA Euro 2008 quarter-final game against Germany.

TRICKY CUSTOMERS

Soccer players spend hours training hard with the squad. The most gifted players also use their time on the training ground to figure out and practice new tricks. Back flicks and step-overs are great to watch at a game. Managers insist that players come up with a result though, such as a goal or an assist for a goal.

NOT A "SHOW PONY"

Cristiano Ronaldo joined Manchester United in 2003, signing for nearly $20 million. He wore the famous number 7 shirt, once filled by legends such as George Best, Eric Cantona, and David Beckham. Young Ronaldo was accused of showing off with all his skills and flicks, but he quickly adapted his game to England's tough Premiership and won over his critics.

BIG BUCKS TRADE

Ronaldo's 2007–08 season ended with a massive haul of 42 goals in total. A master of practice and technique, he has perfected free kicks from just outside the box. The dazzling winger continues to beat players with a bewildering range of tricks. In 2009, he joined Spanish club Real Madrid, for a record-breaking transfer fee of $129 million.

CELEB BIO

Date of birth February 5, 1985

Place of birth Funchal, Madeira, Portugal

Position Winger

Height 6 ft. (1.85 m)

Biggest achievement Winning the 2007–08 Champions League with Manchester United; being named Man of the Match in the final against Chelsea

Training Sporting Lisbon soccer academy

Inspirational figure Diego Maradona

fact

In 2008 Ronaldo became the first Premier League soccer player ever to be named FIFA World Player of the Year.

"I believe I can win [World Player of the Year] again."

OVERSEAS FLAIR

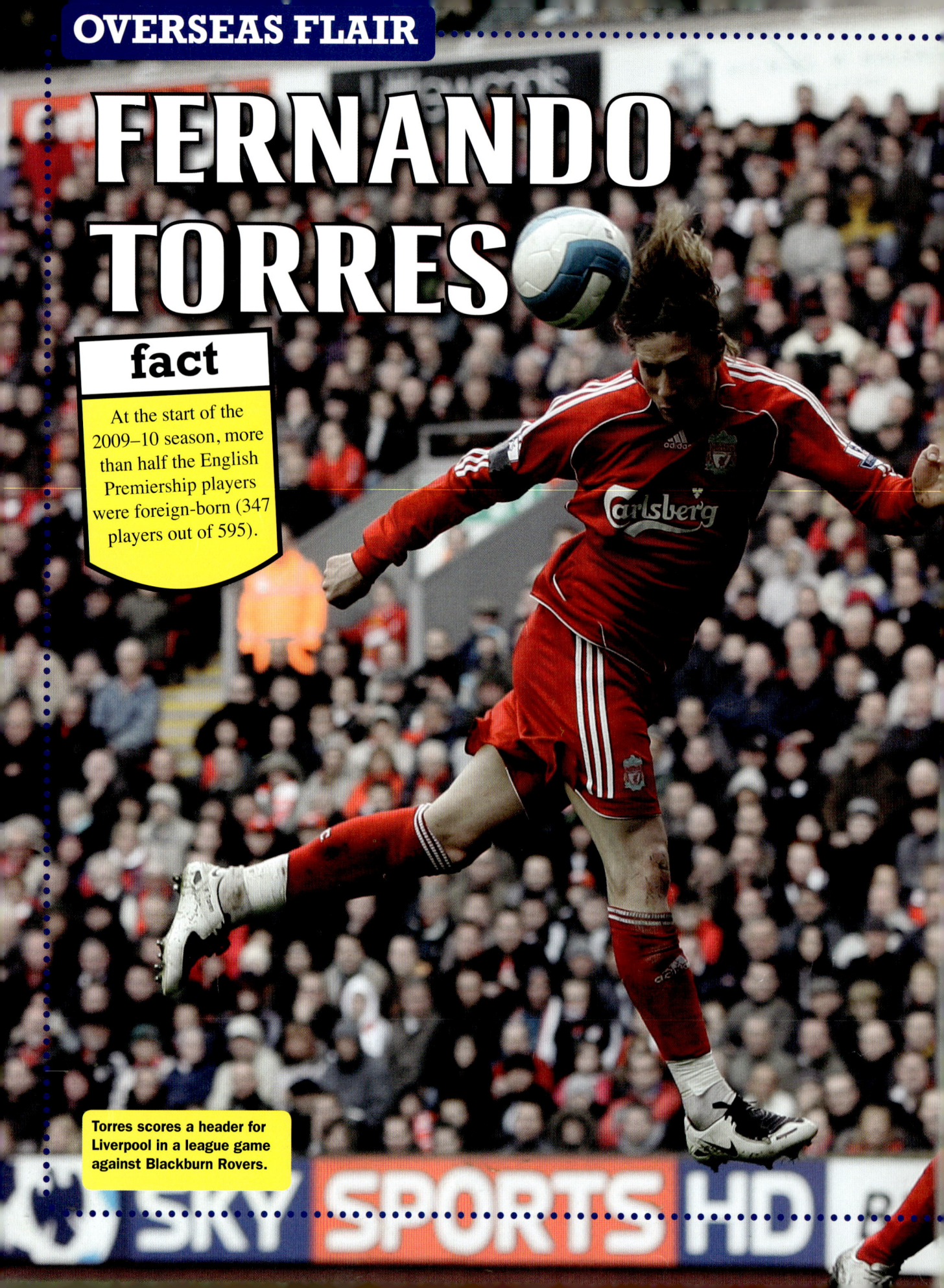

FERNANDO TORRES

fact

At the start of the 2009–10 season, more than half the English Premiership players were foreign-born (347 players out of 595).

Torres scores a header for Liverpool in a league game against Blackburn Rovers.

Some soccer players find it difficult playing for a foreign team. Players like Liverpool's Fernando Torres have to adapt to living abroad and starting at a new club, where everything is different. Some never quite settle in and have to move on again.

OVERSEAS TALENT

Talented new players can boost a squad. Just 22 overseas players featured during the first season of the English Premier League in 1992–93, but over the years, more and more foreign players have graced the Premiership with their skills, including Italian Gianfranco Zola, German Michael Ballack, Frenchman Thierry Henry, and Brazilian Robinho. The influx of foreign soccer players can improve the overall quality of play in a league.

TEAM SUPPORT

Classy Spanish striker Fernando Torres joined Liverpool from Atlético Madrid in 2007. With a Spanish manager and fellow Spaniard Pepe Reina in goal, Torres settled in quickly. His teammates and the fans supported him. Even so, on the playing field he had to adapt to a more physical game than he was used to.

GRIT AND DETERMINATION

Torres relished the challenge. He has pace, guts, and the will to win. A brilliant and cool finisher for club and country, he makes scoring goals look easy. In his first two seasons at Liverpool, Torres scored 50 goals.

PLAYING FOR SPAIN

Torres made his debut for Spain in 2003 against Portugal. Since then he has become a key player for his country, taking part in Euro 2004 and 2008, and the 2006 World Cup. He scored three goals in the World Cup finals and clinched Euro 2008 by scoring the winning goal in the final against Germany.

CELEB BIO

Date of birth **March 20, 1984**
Place of birth **Madrid, Spain**
Position **Striker**
Height **6 ft. 1 in. (1.86 m)**
Biggest achievement **Scoring the only goal in the Euro 2008 final for Spain against Germany**
Training **Atlético Madrid junior teams since age 11**
Inspirational figures **Former Atlético Madrid player Kiko, basketball player Michael Jordan, cyclist Miguel Indurain**

Torres waves his national flag after scoring for Spain in the Euro 2008 final against Germany.

"Upon arriving at a new place, you must want to learn and also be ready to listen to advice."

PLAYING FOR YOUR COUNTRY

WAYNE ROONEY

Playing for a top club is exciting, especially for the lucky soccer players who end up playing for a club they've been a fan of since boyhood. Playing for your country, though, is the highest honor of all.

CLUB VS. COUNTRY

Many good club players never get selected to play for the national team. Others may not shine when playing for their country. It's not just about playing well in big competitions, such as the UEFA European Football (Soccer) Championship and the World Cup. Players have to impress in "friendly" games as well.

BOY WONDER

At just 16, Wayne Rooney burst onto the soccer scene. Playing for Everton, he scored a breathtaking, banana-kick game-winner against Arsenal to become the youngest goalscorer in Premier League history. England had a new star in the making.

ENGLAND REGULAR

With the spotlight on him, Rooney developed into a regular in the England team. An exciting player with great strength and determination, he has proved a hit with England fans. Rooney was injured before the 2006 World Cup and his weak performance contributed to England's early exit from the tournament. Two years later, England failed to qualify for Euro 2008. This disappointment drives Rooney onward.

STRENGTH TO STRENGTH

Rooney is an explosive, physical presence on a soccer field. Developing his skills with Manchester United, he will continue to improve. He has already set his sights on breaking another of Manchester United legend's record—Bobby Charlton's 49 goals for England.

CELEB BIO

Date of birth October 24, 1985

Place of birth Croxteth, Liverpool, UK

Position Striker

Height 5 ft. 10 in. (1.78 m)

Claim to fame Becoming youngest player for England ever at the age of 17 in 2003. (Since then, Theo Walcott broke the record.)

Biggest achievement Winning both the Premiership and the Champions League in 2007–08 with Manchester United

Training Everton Academy starting at the age of 10

Inspirational figures Former Everton player Duncan Ferguson, and United teammates Ryan Giggs and Paul Scholes

England's Rooney shoots during a 2010 World Cup qualifying game against Belarus.

"To play for your country is something which I'm extremely proud of... it's a great honor for me and my family."

fact

Peter Shilton, England goalkeeper between 1970 and 1990, holds the record number of appearances for his country. He has 125 caps.

THE WORLD CUP

RONALDO

The FIFA World Cup is soccer's ultimate prize. Nations play qualifying games to earn the right to compete every four years. The 2006 World Cup final between Italy and France was watched by 715 million people.

fact

Brazil is the most successful country in the history of the World Cup. It's won the competition five times—in 1958, 1962, 1970, 1994, and 2002.

WORLD CUP FINALS

Every four years, a different country is chosen to host the World Cup. Over a period of a month, 32 national teams play in eight different groups, followed by dramatic elimination games. After three games each, the top two teams from each group go forward. Teams then play each other to reach the quarterfinals, semifinals, and final.

O FENOMENO

Ronaldo—short for Ronaldo Luís Nazário de Lima—is a World Cup hero. Like fellow-Brazilian superstar Pelé, he traveled to his first World Cup finals age 17. And, like Pelé, he returned home with the trophy. Nicknamed *O Fenomeno* ("The Phenomenon"), Ronaldo terrorized opposition defenses with his pace and strength. The striker also helped Brazil win the World Cup in 2002.

COMEBACK KID

Ronaldo had a setback in the 1998 World Cup. He could not cope with the pressure of being the team's star and played poorly—Brazil lost the final 3–0 to France. Despite this blow and serious injuries in 1999 and 2000, Ronaldo bounced back for the 2002 World Cup. He was top scorer with eight goals.

Brazilian fans cheer for Ronaldo at the 2002 World Cup in Japan.

"The best player I ever worked with? It has to be Brazil's Ronaldo...lean, mean, and quick as an Olympic sprinter."
FORMER ENGLAND MANAGER, BOBBY ROBSON

CELEB BIO

Date of birth
September 22, 1976

Place of birth
Rio de Janeiro, Brazil

Position **Striker**

Height **6 ft. (1.83 m)**

Claim to fame **At only 16 years of age, he scored 12 goals in 14 games for Brazilian club Cruzeiro in his first season**

Biggest achievement **Becoming the highest goalscorer in the history of the World Cup with a record-breaking 15th goal in 2006**

Training **Sao Cristovao and other local Rio de Janeiro youth teams**

Inspirational figures **Brazil team from 1982 World Cup, including Falcao, Socrates, and Zico**

Ronaldo holds high the World Cup in 2002.

BIG BUCKS

DAVID BECKHAM

fact

David Beckham scored an amazing "Goal of the Season" against Wimbledon in 1996—from the midfield (center) line.

"My career has never been about the money...I've always just wanted to enjoy my soccer [and] play at the top level."

Beckham appears in an ad for a new type of razor.

What do top English players John Terry, Frank Lampard, Steven Gerrard, and Wayne Rooney have in common? They all earn six-figure salaries. That's more than $160,000 a week! But one player, David Beckham, is richer than all of them.

MAKING MONEY

Soccer involves big money. Soccer clubs may spend vast amounts on certain players, but they make their money back by selling tickets and club merchandise, and through deals to televize their games. They also receive sponsorship from big companies that pay to have their names on players' shirts or to advertise at soccer stadiums.

FAMOUS ICON

Global superstar David Beckham, or "Becks," is one of the most famous sports stars in the world. He began his soccer career at Manchester United when he was still a teenager. During his 10 years there, he married pop star "Posh Spice" (Victoria Adams of the Spice Girls), was made captain of the English team, and was runner-up for FIFA World Player of the Year twice. Thanks to his talent and good looks, he became a sports icon.

DRESS SENSE... AND BUSINESS SENSE

As a stylish, fashionable man, Beckham has become a well-known "brand." He earns a lot of money by endorsing sports names, such as Adidas. He also models clothes, sunglasses, and wristwatches. David Beckham went to the top of soccer's "rich list" in 2009 with a fortune of $234 million. His most successful playing days may be behind him, but he is still a star.

Beckham playing for England against Kazakhstan in a qualifying game for the 2010 World Cup.

CELEB BIO

Date of birth **May 2, 1975**

Place of birth **Leytonstone, Greater London, UK**

Position **Midfielder**

Height **6 ft. (1.83 m)**

Biggest achievement **Winning a unique triple of Premier League, FA Cup, and Champions League in 1998–99 with Man. Utd.**

Training **Signed schoolboy forms for Man. Utd. age 14; youth training scheme contract age 16**

Inspirational figures **Bryan Robson, Nelson Mandela, Muhammad Ali**

SHOWBIZ LIFESTYLE

LANDON DONOVAN

Top soccer players are appreciated for their skills on the playing field. These days, many of the most famous players are also known for their showbiz lifestyles and glamorous companions.

MLS GLORY

Landon Donovan is one of the most exciting soccer talents to come out of the U.S. Born in California in 1982, he started playing soccer at just six years of age and hasn't looked back. After a short spell with German club Bayer Leverkusen, Donovan returned to California to play on loan for the San Jose Earthquakes in American MLS (Major League Soccer). Following six years with the club, he moved to another MLS club, LA Galaxy, in 2005.

FAME BECKONS

Donovan's goals helped take the San Jose Earthquakes to the MLS Cup championships twice in three years, and Donovan was named American Soccer Athlete of the Year in both 2003 and 2004. Success on the field led to fame off of it. Donovan won a high-profile sponsorship deal with Nike and became a regular at movie premieres and award ceremonies. On New Year's Eve 2006, Donovan consolidated his celebrity status when he married Bianca Kajlich, star of TV show *The Rules of Engagement*.

HEARTBREAK AND TRIUMPH

Donovan and Kaljich made a glamorous couple, but in private their relationship struggled. They separated in 2009 and filed for divorce in 2010. Despite personal setbacks, Donovan's soccer career has flourished. His MLS success has been matched by his success at international level, where Donovan has become a vital part of the American soccer team. His two goals in the 2010 World Cup made Donovan the highest-scoring American soccer player in World Cup history.

Landon Donovan in action for MLS team LA Galaxy.

"I love winning and any team I'm on, I expect to win."

Landon Donovan and Bianca Kaljich at an awards ceremony.

CELEB BIO

Name **Landon Donovan**

Date of birth **March 4, 1982**

Place of birth **Ontario, California**

Position **Forward**

Height **5 ft. 8 in. (1.73 m)**

Claim to fame **Being four-time winner of American Soccer Male Athlete of the Year**

Biggest achievement **Becoming the USA's top goal scorer**

Inspirational figures **Jurgen Klinsmann, Cobi Jones**

fact

Donovan once nearly had his feet bitten off by an alligator when he was playing golf with his manager!

ROLE MODELS
SAMUEL ETO'O

Eto'o in the Ugandan capital, Kampala, at a soccer school for local schoolchildren.

fact

Samuel Eto'o has scored more goals in the history of the African Nations Cup than any other player.

Today, some soccer players are more like pop idols than sports players. We see them on TV and read a lot about them, but do soccer players make good role models? Cameroon international Samuel Eto'o certainly does!

ON AND OFF THE PLAYING FIELD

Sometimes players behave badly on the field. Some dive to get a free kick or a vital penalty, push the referee, or even start fights. Off the field, many soccer players have gotten drunk and gotten into trouble. Some have crashed their top-of-the-range sports cars.

DOING GOOD

Playing soccer at the highest level brings great wealth and success. This can go to some players' heads. Others, like Samuel Eto'o, use their unique position to promote worthwhile causes and charities. Eto'o is a world-class striker. In his first five seasons with Barcelona, he scored more than 100 goals.

MAKING A STAND

Eto'o campaigns against racism in soccer. He once threatened to walk off during a game after abuse from fans. He argues that no one should feel "looked down upon because of the color of their skin." He also believes strongly in doing charity work. He has donated ambulances, set up soccer academies, and helped schools in several African countries.

Eto'o playing for Barcelona.

CELEB BIO

Date of birth March 10, 1981
Place of birth Douala, Cameroon
Position Striker
Height 5 ft. 11 in. (1.8 m)
Claim to fame Playing for Cameroon against Costa Rica in 1996 age only 14
Biggest achievement Scoring for Barcelona in two Champions League finals—in 2006 against Arsenal and in 2009 against Manchester United
Training Real Madrid youth system
Inspirational figure Roger Milla, Cameroon striker and star of the 1990 World Cup

"Having millions of people watch you play and be influenced by what you do is a huge responsibility. I consider it to be a great honor."

WOMEN'S SOCCER

Women's and girls' soccer is getting bigger and better all the time. More female players compete than in any other sport. Around the world, more than 26 million women and girls are getting out there playing soccer.

fact
Marta played in 103 matches for Swedish side Umea IK—and scored a staggering 111 goals!

MARTA VIEIRA DA SILVA

LIVING IN AMERICA
Probably the planet's biggest female soccer star is the Brazilian Marta Vieira da Silva. If you want a replica shirt you won't need 18 letters though—she is known simply as "Marta." Marta had four successful seasons at top Swedish club Umea IK (2004–08), winning several championships in a row. She then moved to American team Los Angeles Sol.

BRILLIANT BRAZILIAN
Marta is respected worldwide for her dribbling and shooting skills. She has won two Olympic silver medals for Brazil. At the age of 20, Marta became FIFA Women's World Player of the Year in 2006. She went on to keep the trophy in 2007...and 2008!

ON THE UP
Compared to 1993, 15 times as many girls and women are now involved in leagues, cups, and competitions. In the U.S., Women's Professional Soccer (WPS), the top level professional women's soccer league, began to play on March 29, 2009, with seven teams for its first two seasons. There are plans for expansion.

AYSO
The American Youth Soccer Organization (AYSO) is a national, nonprofit organization providing soccer training for children age 4–19 in all 50 states. Now one of the largest single youth sports organizations in the U.S. it has 650,000 players. Watch for star female (and male) players of the future!

CELEB BIO
Date of birth February 19, 1986
Place of birth Dois Riachos, Alagoas, Brazil
Position Striker
Height 5 ft. 4 in. (1.62 m)
Claim to fame Winning a gold medal in the 2003 Pan-American Games, age just 17
Biggest achievement First woman to be voted Women's World Player of the Year by FIFA three times in a row
Training Rio club, Vasco da Gama
Inspirational figure Brazilian striker Rivaldo

"This game has given me so many great moments of joy."

Marta battles for the ball in the Brazil–Germany final of the Women's World Cup in 2007.

FANS' FAVORITES

RYAN GIGGS

Soccer clubs would be nothing without their fans. They follow their club's team through thick and thin, and most fans have a favorite player. Soccer players like Ryan Giggs, who play for the same club for years, have a special relationship with their fans.

DEVOTED FANS

Many soccer fans have a season ticket for their favorite team. They wear replica soccer shirts. Some help write club fanzines or they blog soccer fan sites and web sites with news and views on players and games.

LIFTING THE TEAM

Fans will try to lift their team, so Premiership games are famous for their passion, energy, and noise. Silent, empty stadiums suddenly fill up on game days, tense with excitement. A deafening roar erupts when a player scores—and fans chant his name.

ONE-CLUB HERO

Welsh wizard Ryan Giggs is loved by his army of fans. He joined Manchester United as a youngster and since then has played in more than 800 games for the team. He also plays for Wales. It is rare that a good player stays with one team. Successful players usually move from team to team in pursuit of greater success and higher wages.

THE RIGHT DECISION

Giggs's loyalty has been rewarded by winning many honors with England's top team—including 10 Premiership titles and the Champions League in 1999 and 2008. For Manchester United fans, this one-club hero is a living legend.

> "I had a great reception from the crowd and that gives you an extra lift, an extra buzz."

Giggs playing his last game for Wales in 2007.

fact

On Valentine's Day one year, Ryan Giggs received more than 6,000 cards.

CELEB BIO

Date of birth **November 29, 1973**

Place of birth **Cardiff, Wales, UK**

Position **Winger**

Height **5 ft. 11 in. (1.8 m)**

Claim to fame **Becoming PFA Young Player of the Year 1992 in his first full season—and repeating the feat in 1993**

Biggest achievement **Winning the triple in 1998–99 (see page 19); being BBC Sports Personality 2009**

Training **Manchester City School of Excellence, then Manchester United apprenticeship**

Inspirational figures **Bryan Robson and Nelson Mandela**

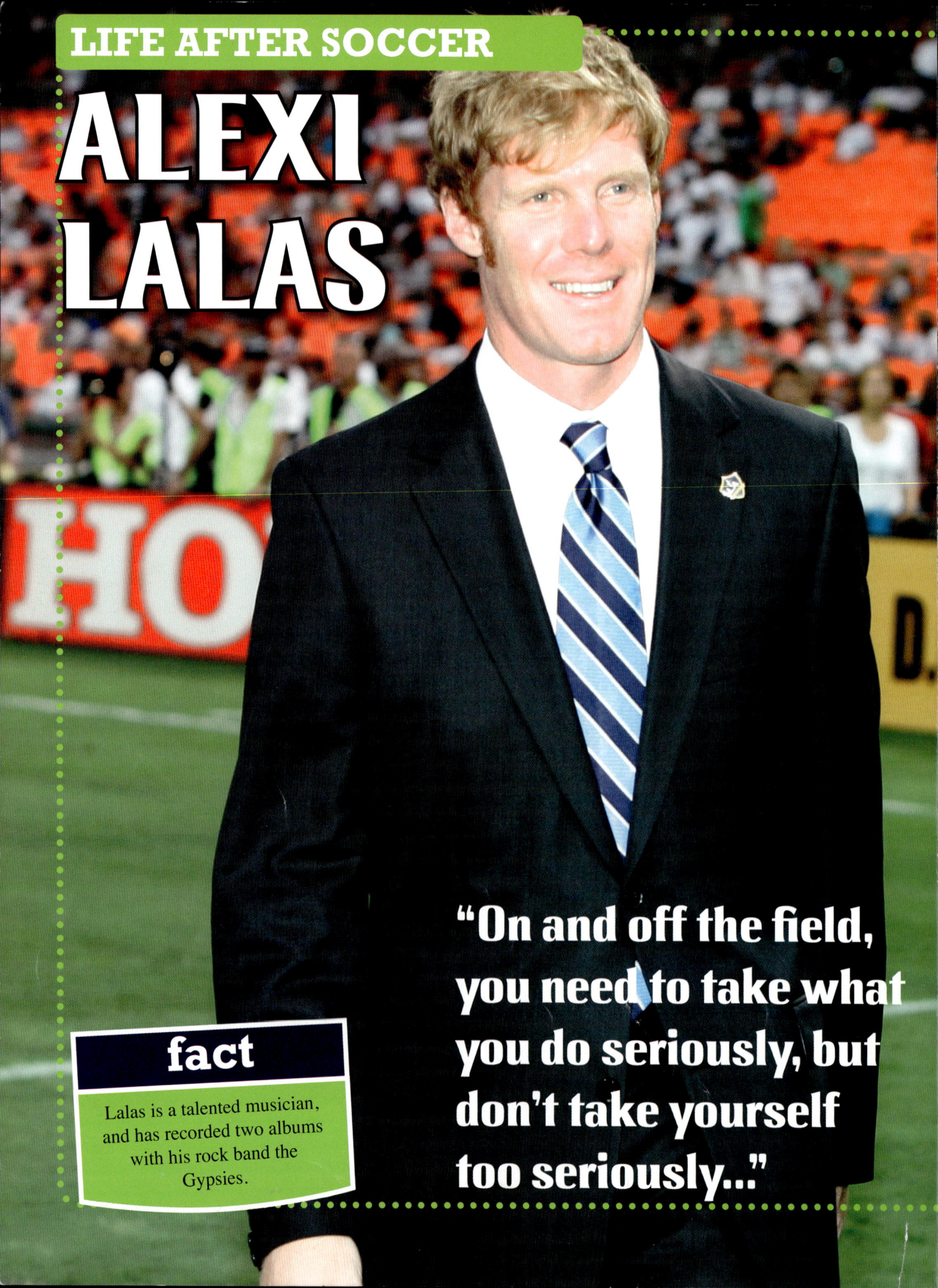

LIFE AFTER SOCCER
ALEXI LALAS

fact

Lalas is a talented musician, and has recorded two albums with his rock band the Gypsies.

"On and off the field, you need to take what you do seriously, but don't take yourself too seriously..."

Is there life after a successful playing career? Most soccer players have a fairly short career of 10 to 15 years. But how can they get the same sort of excitement—the highs and lows—from another job?

STAYING IN SOCCER

Most retired soccer players wish to continue with the game in some way. Some offer their knowledge and expert opinion to the media. Others opt to become coaches and managers. American soccer legend Alexi Lalas has pursued successful careers in both!

PLAYING CAREER

A natural athlete, Lalas excelled in soccer at college and was picked to represent the United States at international level in 1991. Lalas won an amazing 96 caps for his country, and became one of the most recognizable figures in soccer with his bright red hair and beard. The U.S. did not have its own soccer league until the MLS was formed in 1996, so Lalas pursued his playing career abroad. He played for English club Arsenal's reserve team in 1992, and signed for the Italian club Padova in Serie A in 1994. In 1996, Lalas joined the MLS, with spells at New England Revolution, Kansas City Wizards, and LA Galaxy. He announced his retirement from the game in 2004.

MANAGEMENT AND MEDIA

Lalas moved quickly into management, taking up the position of general manager of MLS team the San Jose Earthquakes in 2004 when he was just 33. From there he moved around, ending up at LA Galaxy in 2006, where he helped negotiate David Beckham's famous transfer to the club. He was fired from his position in 2008, but remains involved in soccer, commentating on games for sports channels ESPN and ABC Sports.

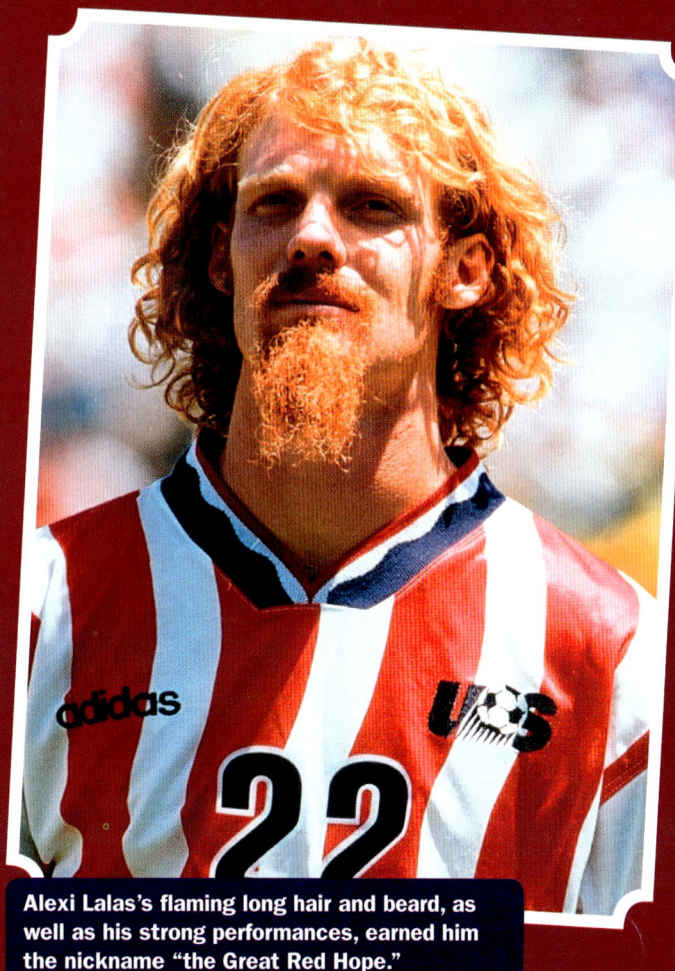

Alexi Lalas's flaming long hair and beard, as well as his strong performances, earned him the nickname "the Great Red Hope."

CELEB BIO

Date of birth **June 1, 1970**

Place of birth **Birmingham, Michigan**

Position **Defender**

Height **6 ft. 3 in. (1.91 m)**

Claim to fame **Becoming the first American soccer player to play in Serie A in Italy**

Biggest achievement **Earning 96 caps for the American national team between 1991 and 1998**

Inspirational figures **Brad Friedel, Jozy Altidore, Bora Milutinovic (former USA manager)**

GLOSSARY

abuse Bad treatment by someone.

AFC Short for Amateur Football Club.

apprenticeship Learning a job or trade from a skilled employer.

assist Pass or cross the ball to a player enabling them to score.

back flick A move where the soccer player passes the ball using the heel of his or her foot.

brand A recognized product or range of products, or a celebrity who endorses such products.

campaign To systematically fight toward achieving a particular aim.

cap an honor earned by a player in recognition of each time he or she has played in an international game for his or her country.

center of excellence A special training school.

club A team that plays in a league.

debut First appearance or game.

defender A player who is positioned to defend the goal and goalkeeper. Defense usually consists of a left back, right back, and two center backs.

discipline Strict rules for behavior.

dribbling Using the feet to closely control the ball in order to run past the other team's players.

dynamic Bursting with energy.

fanzine Fan magazine.

FIFA Short for *Fédération Internationale de Football Association*; the organization that runs international soccer and that is in charge of the FIFA World Cup.

football The name for soccer everywhere in the world except the United States and Canada.

friendly A game that is not a competitive cup or league game.

hat trick (1) When a player scores three goals in a single game. (2) Three wins in a row.

icon Symbol or image.

influx The arrival of many people or things.

inspirational Able to inspire others to do special things.

media The ways to communicate news, such as TV, newspapers, and web sites.

midfielder A player who is positioned in the middle of the playing field as a link between the offensive and defensive players. Most teams play a left, center, and right midfield.

MLS Major League Soccer; the U.S. outdoor professional soccer league established in 1995.

motivate To stimulate interest.

PFA Short for Professional Footballers' Association.

professional Someone who does a job for a living.

racism Discrimination against or abuse of people because of their race.

replica shirt A mass-produced sports jersey or T-shirt that looks just like a player's shirt.

role model Someone who sets a good example.

schoolboy forms Agreements signed by youngsters age between nine and 16 to train and play for a soccer club at junior level. The forms are renewed every year or every two years, if the club is happy with the young player's progress.

set play A free kick or a corner.

soccer academy A school or college that provides soccer training for young people.

squad All of a club's players, not just the team.

step-over A move where the soccer player steps over the ball while dribbling in order to trick an opponent and change direction.

striker A team's most powerful, highest-scoring forward who plays toward the center of the field.

UEFA (Union of European Football Clubs), it runs European soccer and is in charge of the UEFA European Football Championship, the UEFA Champions League, and the UEFA Cup.

wingers the outside forwards who play to the sides of the strikers and whose main task is to pass the ball to the strikers accurately so they can shoot at the goal. Generally, two wingers and one or two strikers work together to score goals.

youth training scheme A placement for a young person that allows them to receive job training.

FURTHER INFORMATION

BOOKS

American Youth Soccer Organization Official Handbook by Vincent Fortanasce and John Ouelette (Simon & Schuster, 2001)

Dream to Win: David Beckham by Roy Apps (Franklin Watts, 2010)

Dream to Win: Wayne Rooney by Roy Apps (Franklin Watts, 2008)

Goal!: Cup Final Day by David James (Ransom Publishing, 2008)

Soccer Halfback by Matt Christopher (Matt Christopher Sports Classics, 1985)

Soccer Hero by Matt Christopher (Matt Christopher Sports Fiction, 2007)

Soccer: How It Works (The Science of Sports) by Suzanne Bazemore (Sports Illustrated Kids, 2010)

Soccer Star! by Jacqueline Guest (Lorimer, 2010)

The First American Soccer Trivia Book by Jamie Clary (Perfect Paperback, 2007)

Top Trumps: World Football Stars 2 by Tim Dykes and Nick Judd (J. H. Haynes and Co. Ltd., 2008)

Winning Soccer for Girls by Deborah W. Crisfield (Winning Sports for Girls, 2009)

21st Century Lives: World Cup Footballers by Adam Sutherland (Wayland, 2010)

DVDS

Boys from Brazil, presented by John Motson (2 Entertain, 2006)

Dare to Dream: The Story of the U.S. Women's Soccer Team (Starring Liev Schreiber, Mia Hamm, Brandi Chastain and Julie Foudy) (HBO, 2007)

FIFA Fever—Best of the FIFA World Cup (Go Entertain, 2006)

WEB SITES

http://www.firstbasesports.com/index.html
A site where you can order instructional books on soccer covering information about basic rules of the game, what to look for during play, league and playoff formats, players and teams of the past and present, and explanations of statistics. You can also find a complete glossary of soccer terms on the site.

http://www.mlssoccer.com
The official site of American Major League Soccer, with all the news about standings, clubs, statistics, and players, and videos to watch.

www.womensleaguesoccer.com/
The official site of Women's Major League Soccer.

www.soccer.org
Site of the American Youth Soccer Association (AYSO).

http://www.goal.com/en
Soccer web site packed with interesting soccer news and information.

www.fifa.com/worldcup/index.html
The official web site of the FIFA World Cup.

http://news.bbc.co.uk/sport1/hi/football/
Latest soccer news, results, fixtures, tables from all around the world, including transfer updates.

31

INDEX

advertising 18, 19
African Nations Cup 22
American Youth Soccer Organization (AYSO) 24, 31
awards
   FIFA Women's World Player of the Year 24
   FIFA World Player of the Year 11, 19
   FWA Footballer of the Year 29
   PFA Players' Player of the Year 5
   PFA Young Player of the Year 27

Ballack, Michael 13
Beckham, David 10, 18-19, 29
Beckham, Victoria 19
Best, George 10

Cantona, Eric 10
captains 4, 5, 8-9, 19, 29
centers of excellence 7, 24
   see also youth academies/teams
Champions League see UEFA competitions
charity work 22-23
Charlton, Bobby 14

Da Silva, Marta Vieira 24-25
Dalglish, Kenny 8, 9, 29
defenders 5, 21
Donovan, Landon 20-21

Eto'o, Samuel 22-23
Euro 2008 see UEFA competitions
European Cup Winners' Cup 29

FA Cup 9, 19, 21, 27, 29
fans 10, 13, 14, 16, 20, 23, 26-27
Ferdinand, Rio 4
foreign players 12-13
fouls 5, 23

game plans 5, 8
Gerrard, Steven 4, 8-9, 19
Giggs, Ryan 14, 26-27

hat tricks 7
Henry, Thierry 7, 13

Kaljich, Bianca 20, 21
Kiko 13

Lalas, Alexi 28-29
Lampard, Frank 19

managers 5, 8, 10, 13, 20, 28-29
Maradona, Diego 10
midfielders 8, 9, 19, 29, 30

MLS (Major League Soccer) 20, 29, 30

national teams 14-15
   Belarus 14
   Brazil 16, 17
   Cameroon 23
   Costa Rica 23
   Croatia 7
   England 4, 5, 7, 14-15, 19
   France 16
   Germany 10, 13, 25
   Italy 16
   Portugal 7, 10
   Scotland 29
   Spain 13
   USA 20, 29
   Wales 26

Pan-American Games 24
Pelé 16
Premier League
   English Premiership 7, 10, 12, 13, 14, 19, 20, 21, 26, 27
   Scottish 29
   Women's 24

racism 23
Reina, Pepe 13
Rivaldo 24
Robinho 13
Robson, Bobby 16
Robson, Bryan 19, 27
Ronaldo 16-17
Ronaldo, Cristiano 10-11
Rooney, Wayne 14-15, 19

salaries 10, 18-19, 20, 26
Scholes, Paul 14
Serie A 29
Shilton, Peter 15
skills 10-11
soccer clubs 19, 26
   Aberdeen 29
   AC Milan (Italy) 8
   Arsenal 6, 7, 14, 23, 29
   Atlético Madrid (Spain) 13
   Barcelona (Spain) 23
   Blackburn Rovers 12
   Celtic 28, 29
   Chelsea 5, 10
   Coventry 29
   Cruzeiro (Brazil) 17
   Everton 14
   Kansas City Wizards 29
   LA Galaxy 20
   Liverpool 8, 9, 12, 13
   Los Angeles Sol (USA) 24

Manchester United 10, 14, 19, 23, 26, 27, 29
New England Revolution 29
Padova 29
Real Madrid (Spain) 10
San Jose Earthquakes 20, 29
Southampton 7
Umea IK (Sweden) 24
strikers 5, 13, 14, 16, 17, 23, 24, 30

Terry, John 4-5, 19
Torres, Fernando 12-13

UEFA Champions League
   1998-99 19, 26, 27
   2004-05 8, 9
   2005-06 23
   2007-08 5, 10, 14, 26, 28
   2008-09 23
UEFA Cup 9
UEFA European Football Championship 14
   Euro 2008 10, 13, 14
UEFA European Under-21 Championship 7

Walcott, Theo 6-7, 14
wingers 7, 10, 27, 30
women's soccer 24-25
World Cup, FIFA 14, 16-17
   1982 17
   1990 23
   1998 16
   2002 15, 16, 17
   2006 7, 14, 16
   2010 4, 7, 14-15, 19, 20
WPS (Women's Professional Soccer) 24

youth academies/teams 6-7, 22, 23
   AFC Newbury 6, 7
   Arsenal 21
   Atlético Madrid (Spain) 13
   Chelsea 5
   Everton 14
   Liverpool 8, 9
   Manchester City 27
   Manchester United 19, 27
   Real Madrid (Spain) 23
   Sao Cristovao (Brazil) 17
   Southampton 7
   Sporting Lisbon (Portugal) 10
   Swindon Town 7
   Vasco da Gama (Brazil) 24

Zola, Gianfranco 5, 13